The Mist I Was

Dahlia Jones

To my lost ones.

Intangible

After Sharon Van Etten

Because silence sounds like fear and because thirst tastes like

memories-

that is why I remembered.

She has a dusky voice

and she sings whiskey-kissed renderings

of how a heart feels

when I tear the stitches sewn

to connect his heart

with mine like some desperate

silent cry swallowed in angry waves

brought on by hurricanes

and your thinly concealed rage.

She sings folk and plays piano

and all the while

she brings me to you.

Nessuno

I remember the shape Jay's shoulders made silhouetted

against the dark stage behind him at his brother's funeral. He held

himself up on the podium; his body too weak to carry all that grief. I

stared up at him as he recounted between sobs the brief few seconds

that John woke up. When he died again, Jay let him go. There were

no words left, only bitter, suffocated hyperventilation. Afterwards,

everyone sang, raised their hands above their heads, rocked side-to-

side, and cried out: "Lord!", and I thought: What could supplication

possibly do for any of you?

I looked up at John so pale in that satin-lined box on the stage- bathed in blue and white lights and I wondered how praying and crying to god would help anyone with their oppressive longing and loss. I noted the forced, peaceful looks in his parents' faces because the church always told them not to be sad: "After all, he's going to a better place" they soothed themselves with naive hopes and dreams.

I knew then that heaven is just a lie we tell ourselves to make us feel better about the inevitable nothingness of oblivion. I did not sway or sing or pray to god. I stood, eyes fixed on my very real, dead friend lying in his gray coffin and I did not say goodbye-I knew he couldn't hear me.

Silence

You've stapled my lips shut and wonder why I do not speak.

Cotard

Sometimes, if I laugh too hard, I know without a doubt that I am dead. I know that you wrapped your thin, long fingers around my throat and squeezed until I saw black, felt the blood stopped-up in my neck, and unbearable pangs reverberated through my head as you stole my life. You stared into my eyes as they grew more red and watery until they simply stopped examining your completely blank expression.

I know that true happiness such as this is unattainable. It doesn't exist-it is a divine, exquisite dream only guessed at by romantics and poets. No: Happiness such as this-love such as this cannot be real and it cannot be believed because I know I'm dead.

Letter to my Dear Edith

There in my dreams   a child much

aggrieved

for its sweet breath   never to

be drawn-

          such small hands   never to be held

in mine.

                              Dear one,

          I would have loved   to hold you

close

          and see those bright eyes   and little

smiles.

I would have loved you   if

only the world

          and humanity had   changed.

Because I

          cannot protect you from   what has

destroyed me

                    so fully. I would have

loved to love you if only my body had truly

been

mine.

Only People can be Blue Dahlias

Sometimes I see them in my dreams, friends that humbled

me so greatly. I never understood when people told me that I thought

I was invincible- I had no such illusions and indeed, none of us did. I

grew up with them, those blue dahlias-moments that collected

themselves from different years I knew them until the last time I

knew them. Those glances and last words, compartmentalized neatly in my memory, never to be forgotten but seldom examined. Those remembrances are all I have left of them, aside from the irrevocable loss of myself.

No, we knew we would die the moment we saw those people jumping from burning buildings, plummeting towards the earth on bubble-screen TVs in early September. We knew there was no explanation for things when we saw John's body lowered into the ground. I remember how alone his cemetery seemed, how at the edge of civilization it was but when I go back I see how life has moved on without him. Concrete buildings surround him now, completely oblivious to his existence, to the piece of me buried with him, and the white rose I laid on his rain-slick coffin.

I remember Ben even more clearly and vibrantly as if he were an articulated butterfly in a cloche. Little things about him haunt me most: The way he looked wearing yellow, the grey in his blue eyes, and the way that ash cross clung to his forehead. It's those goddamn little things that jolt me awake just like the waves that rippled through me the day I heard he died. All of us hoped that it had been fast, that he had died immediately because he was so badly broken. I think of how beautiful he looked in those Wednesday ashes and how there is nothing left of him but dust in an urn. He reminds me of the sea and whenever I go home to Virginia, I forget there have been entire lives lived since he died.

Cain always said, "I'm gonna die young, I can feel it." He was right of course. Sometimes I think I see him, hidden in crowds. I look up at those sad eyes, full and absent of color simultaneously and I remember his lopsided smile as if he'd never left and I stare for as long as I can until I am forced to blink; to break my focus and then he is gone again until the next time I sit with his memory on a cold morning and we watch the sunrise together.

I remember Fern with her sunlit sapphire eyes and the most electrifying smile I have ever seen. The day she went missing I knew within myself that she was dead, it had all been too much to bear. Sometimes I see her in nightmares; waterlogged, her eyes turned to frosted sea glass, she's a silver streak against the dark pines, and she always asks me from her bed of leaves, "Why didn't you help me?"

Why didn't I help her?

They all haunt me-blue, delicate, and blooming in the void of eternal youth. I see their faces flash in my mind on a slow-reel-their faces before we knew we were vulnerable and afterwards. I think of our teachers in high school and how they watched us become something other than we had been before, something just a little bit darker. They knew that we had become great strangers to ourselves and to each other- a communal loss of innocence bonded us in a sickly sentimental purgatory. We exist as specimens in a jar, still alive but we can't push the lid off as desperately as we try. We drown slowly in sorrow and grasp at anything and everything to make us meaningful. I don't know when I stopped understanding myself or if indeed I ever did.

Only After I Forget do

I find us by the sea,

still I feel your warmth and still

beats my heart to your pulse.

Your eyes are all the colors I can't see-

radiant, they cut me to the bone.

See, my love, we ache the same.

I can find us in the sea,

honey-blue waves wash me clean

lift the illusion of time

I suffocated beneath.

After all these years,

        my heart still searches for you.

One Day I'll Find the Right Words

Ink has failed me almost entirely where tears have never let me down. If I dipped my pen in my bruise-colored glitter tears, they could capture you-press you to this paper and preserve the colors I am with you. You make me that antique orange in sunsets-vibrant and muted-impossible to keep when painted and it always, no matter what, turns dark when the light fades.

Trazodone

If I eat these pills that take me away

and you spin me just right

and my muscles remember how to

move with you;

if I dance with you in this hot room

and the lighting is dark enough

I'll feel it for a few seconds-

my dark mind stops.

Nothing and no one now,

just me, spinning outside myself

draped in this silver dress

that clings to my skeleton just right.

Just right-

no noise, no counting, no hunger

only pure silence spun to the end of the record

until the needle catches

until I feel how close I am

to starving to death

and if it wasn't for these pills

that take me away

I could focus on something

-anything but those few seconds

of nothingness and

silence.

The Name on the Cover is not Mine but I've Signed My Life in

These Lines

It always made me sad

to see the remains of

what once was art.

Discarded,

shed

like snake skins-

their names scribbled-

artists claiming nothing

and yet, they made me feel.

Vapor

       I don't know why

       but I see a ghost

       in a boy I know

       and I can't help but

       stare at him sometimes

       and he lets me linger

       longer than I should-

       stunned and speechless

       at how similar

he is to someone

already dead.

I Know More than I can Articulate

I wake up running

in a house that never ends.

I cannot trust anything

and I cannot stop not even

to breathe, not even

to think clearly but still

I

try to find the logic

of it all but I fall

on the

Slipping dirt of this place

Never can I find my feet

                          still on a solid surface.

                                              I

am transported to

                          another room and each

one feels like I've been

                          there before and I know I'm

searching eternally for someone.

                    I catch glimpses- flashes

                                        bright and

welcoming like

              an oil-burning lamp and

                                    just for a moment-

the ground stops shifting.

                                              time

ends just for

                          A few brief seconds.

                    Just as fast as before

                                        the floor crumbles

beneath me

        I'm breathless, panting, and

                                searching endlessly

for the glow of an

                        oil-burning lamp

and all the warmth

                        I have craved

        but never felt

                -forever.

Green Dreams

Lavender flavored smoke or

lilac

fills my lungs

soft tendrils caressing me

I wonder--

can it feel loneliness?

Maybe that's why it touches

me so tenderly,

gently

-then leaves me

coughing and sore.

When I let what's left

of it's love go

I'm acrid

and it's

angry.

It always makes me float

but it leaves me

too soon:

My lover that

knows me too well.

I cherish it above the rest

since you've gone

away like all the ones

before but at least

I can always get more.

I Can Never Tell the Difference Between Daydreams and

Hallucinations

The sky, like a peeled muscle,

        wrings itself out on the windshield.

I like to drive west at midnight;

        when the rivers are coiled silver snakes,

and the world is asleep.

        I thought

if I could drive fast enough far enough,

        I could outrun you.

But you found me

        -startled me,

like the back half of an autumn breeze.

        Not the crisp, exciting part,

the part that whispers:

You shouldn't be here.

We sit in my piece of shit Ford

 while Billie Holiday croons her soft power

into the space between us:

 Gloomy Sunday on a good friday.

You look at me

 with spectral eyes

like small black stones.

 There's a lot of things I need to say

but for right now,

 I think I'll just keep pretending

that you're really here.

Dissociations in the Dark

Dahlias come in many colors,

but blue is not one of them,

I think to myself as your

knuckles crack against my face.

My lip splits open-

my under eyes are purple and black.

Wilted petals fall to the floor.

Stems curl and dry; they refuse

to take in water.

The corpses of my favorite dahlias-

the kind that don't exist-

drop from an empty vase.

They hit the floor and I join them.

If you spoke kindly to them,

they would revive,

but they aren't real,

so you don't speak to them,

and they do not bloom.

I would rather cease to be,

and you could have the flowers instead.

Fields of deep blue dahlias to take my place-

what a beautiful memorial.

Would you speak kindly then,

if I did not exist?

How to Find Forever

Heaven is a marsh dock on the edge of everything.

I know because I've been there

-because that's where I go to talk to Cain on

cold mornings in Virginian mountains

where I made paradise in my mind

while dancing on the edge of some blue ridge.

     I always know when I'm dreaming and just like

everyone, I love to believe my own lies.

     So I walk through thick, opalescent vapor-

brilliant, scattered sunlight refracted a million

     ways and time dies in this shimmering vastness

before me and I see two chairs surrounded by oblivion.

     It's colder than I thought it'd be and quiet

-the kind of quiet that belongs to eternity.

     It's calm and peaceful and perfect so quiet

the never-ending noise in my head stops and all

     that's left is Cain and I, and all I feel is free.

Sometimes I hold his hand and we just sit and stare at

     our breath, iridescent clouds reflecting

all the colors of a sunrise over those purple-stained

     hills I love to lose myself in, where I first found

heaven in my mind, in a lucid dream that I want so

desperately to be real but know it can't.

Cain is dead and I can never see him again unless

I choose to dream of him and let his

voice, deep and gently thunderous carry me away

like a silk string tossed on the wind, caught

and twirled til it's frayed and spent, tired and broken

like I am because I can never rest or let go

of memories-of people I lost and I haunt myself

For hours on this dock because I can't say

goodbye. I can't lose him even though I know I

already have. When I inevitably see through my

beautifully crafted story, Cain and me sit in silence and let

a million prisms blind us to the reality that there is

really only one person sitting on the dock in my heaven.

But still; I and everyone else

love to believe our own lies.

What I Left in the Woods

Now she's marble on the forest floor-

her veins are thick, black rivers

and her eyes are stuck open in the

moonlight like pallid pearls.

Her skin puckered and wrinkled

before the water gave her up.

The stream is still caught in her lungs

while maggots writhe on her tongue.

I know I'll see her again-

she'll be always in my nightmares

and her blood-caked face

will twist in recognition

when she sees me; an old friend.

Branches whip my face as

I tear through the woods, blood

coats my teeth and I'm breathless, just like her.

Tears spatter decaying leaves.

I escape her every time but

when I wake up I know

I'll wish I'd stayed.